Families

Role Models

Revised Edition

Rebecca Rissman

Heinemann Library
Chicago, Illinois

www.capstonepub.com
Visit our website to find out
more information about
Heinemann-Raintree books.

To order:

☎ Phone 800-747-4992

🖥 Visit www.capstonepub.com
to browse our catalog and order online.

Edited by Rebecca Rissman and Catherine Veitch
Designed by Ryan Frieson
Picture research by Tracy Cummins
Originated by Capstone Global Library Ltd
Printed in the United States of America in Eau Claire, Wisconsin.
052015   009034RP

**Library of Congress Cataloging-in-Publication Data is
available on the Library of Congress website.**
  ISBN 9781484668344 (pb)

Acknowledgments
We would like to thank the following for permission to reproduce
photographs: Getty Images: Absodels, 22, Chip Somodevilla,
21, Colin Hawkins, 19, digitalskillet, 7, Don Mason, 10, Grady
Reese, 5, Hill Street Studios, 14, 23 middle, Hoptocopter, 17,
Jim Bastardo, 15, Joeleen Pryhitko, 16, Juergen Frank/Corbis/
VCG, 13, LWA, cover, Michael Regan, 11, Uwe Krejci, 12, Zoran
Milich, 20, 23 top; Shutterstock: Alena Brozova, back cover, 6,
bikeriderlondon, 9, Juice Dash, 8, Monkey Business Images, 4, 18,
23 bottom

We would like to thank Anne Pezalla and Nancy Harris for their
invaluable help in the preparation of this book.

Every effort has been made to contact copyright holders of
any material reproduced in this book. Any omissions will
be rectified in subsequent printings if notice is given to
the publisher.

Contents

What Is a Family?

A family is a group of people who care for each other.

Families can be very different.

Families can be very special.

Families can be large or small.

What Are Families Like?

Families can be loud.

Families can be quiet.

What Is a Role Model?

Role models are leaders.

They make other people want to do
what they do.

Role models set a good example.

They show others how to do the
right thing.

Role Models in the Family

Family members can be role models.

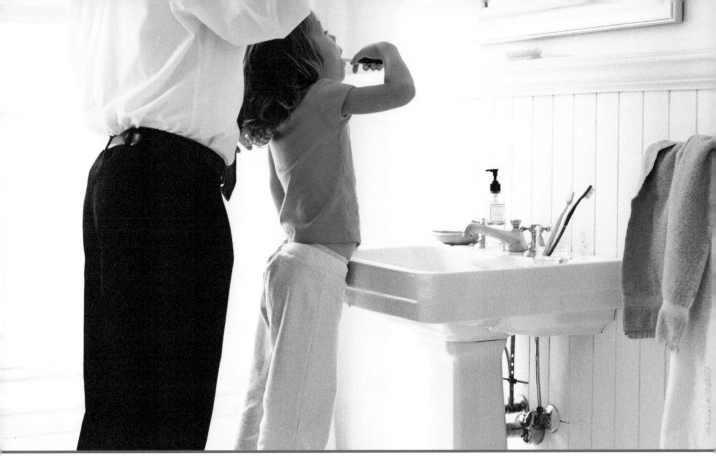

Parents can be role models.

Brothers and sisters can be
role models.

Grandparents can be role models.

Role Models Outside of the Family

People who are not family members can be role models.

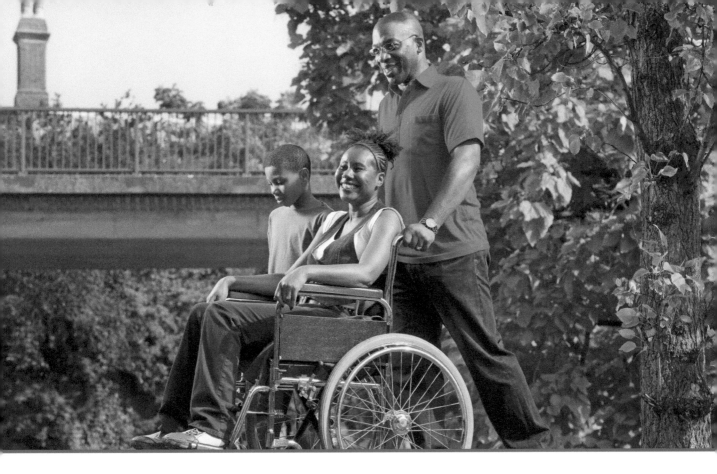

Friends can be role models.

Teachers and coaches can be role models.

Even people you do not know can
be role models.

Your Role Model

Do you have a role model?

Can you be a role model?

Picture Glossary

 **coach** person who helps others learn about a sport or game

 **member** person who belongs to a group

 **teacher** person who helps others learn. Teachers often work at schools.

Index

Note to Parents and Teachers
Before Reading
Write "Leader" and "Good Example" on the board, and ask children to come up with descriptive words for each. Record the descriptors under the two words. Then discuss how a good role model is a good leader and sets a good example.

After Reading
Ask children to make a poster showing a role model they know. Encourage them to cut out words and pictures from magazines that help describe their role model. Then ask children to turn their poster over, and use the opposite side for a role model they don't know, such as President Obama. Encourage them to use magazine clippings on this poster as well.